Power, Love, and a Sound Mind

Freedom From Anxiety, Fear and Other
Destructive Thinking!
2 Timothy 1:7

Disclaimer: The information in this book is not intended to address any form of mental illness and does not discount or replace the need for medical advice.

Table of Contents

Second Edition: January 2019

Foreword

The information in this book should/could be studied when there is no anxiety, fear, etc., in order to be prepared if/when these conditions arise.

Introduction

Often times when you want to attack an area of your life such as freedom from anxiety or freedom from whatever you may be struggling with, just getting started is the first step of the battle. I thought it might be helpful to start this book with what is called a "starter prayer". This is a simple prayer to help you get your eyes off of what you are struggling with and onto the living God. So, here we go:

> Heavenly Father, You know what I am struggling with and what I am facing. You know my weaknesses. But, today I will be transformed and renew my mind. I fix my mind on You. I submit myself to You and Your Word. My thoughts are on You and the love You have for me. Thank You for the grace and mercy you shower over me. Thank You for the sacrifice Your Son made for me on the cross so that I may have everlasting life. Thank you for the gift of your Holy Spirit and the peace and hope that fills me. I now receive Your unconditional love, peace and hope for me as I proceed. In Jesus' name, Amen.

Be anxious for nothing, but in everything by
prayer and supplication, with thanksgiving,
let your requests be made known to
God; and the peace of God, which surpasses

Chapter 1 - Putting First Things First

Lessons Learned While on the Backside of the Desert

I will never forget the day that I called my good friend who was a registered nurse living in my area at the time. I had been struggling with tremendous back pain, and, on several occasions, had a difficult time catching my breath while doing normal, everyday things. I had been to several doctors trying to determine the cause of the back pain, heart palpitations and breathing difficulties. I had even had an angiogram. (Glory to God, all of the tests came back negative.) But, on that day, after a rather severe episode, I called my friend and said, "I think I'm having an anxiety attack!" As she listened to me intently, she looked up the word *anxiety* in her nurse's manual. As she read the definition to me, I nearly fainted. Yep! It described exactly what I was experiencing.

There are several definitions for the word *anxiety*. But I will use the one that I remember coming from my friend's nurse's manual. I learned that the word, *anxiety*, is derived from the Latin word, *angere*, and it means, *to choke*, or *to strangle*. And that is exactly what I was experiencing! It was as if something were choking me. And do you know what? It was! At the time, I did not know what it was, or how to recognize it, but I was under a severe attack, and it was the *anxiety* that was choking me!

I have loved God ferociously since I was 20 years old and got *radically saved* on Ohio State's Campus in Columbus, Ohio. (*Saved* as described in the Bible. Please see "Salvation Through Christ" at the back of this book.)

Though being saved as a young 20 year old and knowing that God was now living in my heart, I did not realize at the time, that that same God was *so willing* to help me with this *anxiety*. Somehow along the journey, I thought that I had to do this, and many other things, on my own.

It was hard for me to ask for help in the beginning of my journey. I worked hard in college. When times got tough, I would pull myself up by my own bootstraps and handle them. I was a strong college student and thought *hard work* and *striving* were just the way things were. Little did I realize, that the *hard work* and *striving* and *climbing*, had me climbing a very *dangerous, self-ambitious* ladder. It was only a matter of time, before God had to show me that *this* (working oneself into a frenzy to get ahead) is NOT the way of Christianity. God's way is one of FAITH, GRACE, TRUST, and REST. God's way is being able to *discover* what He has placed within you for *His purposes* and *allow* those gifts to flow out of you! "For we are His workmanship, created in Christ Jesus for good works, which God prepared beforehand that we should walk in them." (Ephesians 2:10, NKJV)

This does not mean you will not work because, believe me, you will. But, you will be working from a different vantage point. You will work from a vantage point of *God's* strength, and not your own.

Back to my story - In my early 30s and as the *ladder climbing* continued, I was very happily married and my husband and I were wild about our 2 young children. (I am *still* wild about my husband and our, now, grown children, today.) But back then, little by little, I found myself beginning to spin one plate after another. Before one project and/or demand would end, I was saying "yes" to yet another, without, at times, even finishing the first one. Even worse, I was not asking our Lord whether or not He was even *in* all of those projects in the first place.

But, there I was, with a fervent passion for God, a passion for Bible Studies (both teaching and attending them), running a household, and dealing with the demands of two young children and having my husband, due to his job, often traveling out of the country, I was endeavoring to do it all.

I was spinning more and more of those plates. Eventually, the plates became too many, too fast, and too furious for me to bear, and they began to fall and break. And, you guessed it. As *they* began to break, so did I!

One day, the final plate (the one that prompted me to call my nurse friend) fell crumbling to the floor and I went with it. At the time, I was desperately trying to get out of the door with my two little ones, their snacks, my Bible books and notebooks, purse, and who knows what else, and I simply could not get my breath. I remember, also, that my back hurt so badly. It was not, however, that *usual* backache with which I had become all too familiar. This ache drove me to my knees. So, before making it out of the door, I literally fell to my family room floor, lying flat on my back. I began to weep and remember thinking, "I just need some help! I can't do it all!"

As the tears began streaming down my face, I began to cry out to God. I will never forget the dialogue that I had with Him while there on that floor. I said, "God, I can't do anything. I can't go to my meetings. I can't meet one-on-one with anyone. I can't do these things for You." What happened next was the surprise of my life - one of the most incredible *defining moments* that has helped to shape me into the person I am today. I felt one of the strongest impressions on the inside of me from the Holy Spirit that I have ever had. As I, in angst, was pouring out my heart to God saying that I could not do another single activity for Him that day, He whispered one single word. He simply said, *"Finally!"* I remember lying there thinking, "What? *Finally?*"

This was a lesson that God had been trying to get over to me all along. But I was always too busy to see or hear Him. As I soon learned, my issue, as I lay there on the floor that day, was much more than a *physical* problem. It was a *spiritual* one.

But, my friends, that spiritual problem turned into a life-changing 3-year journey of discovering God. Yes, I was saved, but I had so much to learn. And those 3 years were the beginning of my learning and growing. I call those years *the backside of the desert years*. I will cherish them forever. They gave me experiences with God that have changed my life forever.

As I was taken from the hamster's wheel back then, and placed onto the Potter's wheel, it became apparent to me that I was trying to do things *for* God without really *knowing* Him. Things had to change and, by His mercy and grace, they did change. During those three years, through my journey, I learned:

- Who the Lord is, His character, His nature – God is full-on love. (1 John 4:8)
- Just *how much* He loves me (which is one of the crucial revelations to walking in freedom from anxiety). (John 3:16)
- That I was saved by grace and not works. (Ephesians 2:8-10).
- That God truly did have a plan for my life and it was/is a good plan! (Jeremiah 29:11, Matthew 11:28)

What I did not mention earlier, but absolutely must include, is, that during the crumbling plates and crumbling 'Anna', time, fear had found its way into my life. Fear, followed by bouts of anxiety had begun to grip my mind and my thought life. I needed help! And as He always does, God came! I always say that He put me into the I.C.U. Unit of the Holy Spirit!

Day after day, night after night, for those three years, I would simply sit with a Bible and notes. I read about God, I worshipped God, and I got to **know** God.

I learned to put the Lord at the *Center* of everything I do. I memorized Matthew 11:28 (NKJV) "Come to Me, all you who labor and are heavy laden, and I will give you rest" and visited it **regularly**. I learned to go back to the cross where all the work of being free from fear, anxiety, and things of this world were **truly taken care of** by Jesus Christ, my Lord and Savior. I learned, and *am still learning*, how to walk in the grace that God has provided. I have learned to enjoy the journey.

As you continue to read, you will see some of the principles, prayers and solutions that have helped me to not only get free, but to remain free. I pray that the same thing will happen for you.

He who does not love does not know God, for God is love.
1 John 4:8 (NKJV)

For God so loved the world that He gave His only begotten Son, that whoever believes in Him should not perish but have everlasting life.
John 3:16 (NKJV)

For by grace you have been saved through faith, and that not of yourselves; it is the gift of God, not of works, lest anyone should boast. For we are His workmanship, created in Christ Jesus for good works, which God prepared beforehand that we should walk in them.
Ephesians 2:8-10 (NKJV)

For I know the thoughts that I think toward you," says the Lord, "thoughts of peace and not of evil, to give you a future and a hope.

*Come to Me, all you who labor and are
heavy laden, and I will give you rest.*
Matthew 11:28 (NKJV)

Chapter 2 - The Lord is My Peace

For God has not given us a spirit of fear, but of power and of love and of a sound mind.
2 Timothy 1:7 (NKJV)

I was already quite familiar with this 2 Timothy 1:7 (NKJV) Scripture. *For God has not given us a spirit of fear, but of power and of love and of a sound mind -* familiar at least in my head. I can remember oftentimes grabbing it in panic, with the thought, "If I say it enough times, like a genie that pops out of Aladdin's lamp, the anxiety and the fear will go away." Little did I realize that Biblical truths are much deeper than that. Biblical truths are just *that* - they are *truths* from God, Himself, to and for you. But they are not meant to only be quick fixes. (Though they will fix the problem.) Rather, they are *God Himself* and they are meant to go deep into who we are and transform us into the very image of Christ.

My job, as I began to discover and unpack 2 Timothy 1:7, was to break down that Scripture, as it is packed with revelation power. I let it get so much on the inside of me that whenever I would have the thought of anxiety, out of my mouth and heart would come this 2 Timothy 1:7 verse.

Before I did that, however, it was crucial for me to have the revelation that God is Peace, *my Peace*, and that the fear that I felt was not given to me by God.

=== **PEACE** ===

So Gideon built an altar there to the Lord,
and called it The-Lord-Is-Peace.
Judges 6:24 (NKJV)

The Lord is Peace is literally *Yahweh Shalom.* The Hebrew word *shalom* means peace, prosperity, completeness, soundness, welfare. *Shalom* covers relationships with God and with people. Biblical *shalom* is the inward sense of completeness or wholeness.

For He Himself is our peace…
Ephesians 2:14 (NKJV)

Peace is ours. Prosperity is ours. Christ is our Peace. The new covenant is based on the finished work of Christ and that includes peace! When salvation (Christ) comes into our lives, the blessing of peace (shalom) comes, also.

----

*Jesus said to him, "I am the way, the truth,
and the life…"*
John 14:6 (NKJV)

There is only one way to peace, and that is through Jesus.

----

*…for the kingdom of God is not eating and
drinking, but righteousness and peace and
joy in the Holy Spirit*
Romans 14:17 (NKJV)

Peace is in the kingdom of God.

----

*But the fruit of the Spirit is love, joy, peace,
longsuffering, kindness, goodness,
faithfulness, gentleness, self-control.*
Galatians 5:22-23 (NKJV)

Peace is a fruit of the Spirit.

I would go over and over these truths, building my faith and building my foundation on Who God is: that God is **Peace** and that **this Peace**, now, lived on the inside of me.

As I continued to build on the truth that Christ is Peace, I knew I then had to deal with the issue of fear. What is the source of fear and how did it get here?

If you look at the very beginning of the Bible in Genesis 3:8, you see that God walked with Adam in the Garden of Eden in the cool of the day. As Adam partook of the fruit of the tree of knowledge of good and evil (from which he was forbidden to take, Genesis 2:17), he sinned. That sin then opened the door for all sin to take place. Along with Adam's fall, came the fear. *So he said, "I heard Your voice in the garden, and **I was afraid** because I was naked; and I hid myself."* (Genesis 3:10, NKJV) [Bold and italics added for emphasis] What was once faith, now turned into fear. What had formerly been a beautiful faith-walk (trusting in, relying on God) transformed into an un-Godly spiritual fear-walk that connected him to the devil.

Fear is twisted or perverted faith. [1]
Faith activates God. [2]
Fear activates Satan. [3]

BUT, if you have accepted Jesus Christ as your Lord and Savior, you <u>are no longer under Adam and that sin he committed</u>. You are under the <u>perfect love of Jesus Christ</u> and the ramifications of Adam's sin (which include fear), no longer need to have a grip on you!

*And because you belong to him, the power of
the life-giving Spirit has freed you from the
power of sin that leads to death.*
Romans 8:2 (NLT)

*Therefore, just as through one man sin
entered the world, and death through sin,
and thus death spread to all men, because all
sinned—*
Romans 5:12 (NKJV)

The Following Verses Provide the Solution
to Romans 5:12

*(...For if by the one man's offense death
reigned through the one, much more those
who receive abundance of grace and of the
gift of righteousness will reign in life through
the One, Jesus Christ.) Therefore, as
through one man's offense judgment came to
all men, resulting in condemnation, even so
through one Man's righteous act the free gift
came to all men, resulting in justification of
life. For as by one man's disobedience many
were made sinners, so also by one Man's
obedience many will be made
righteous. Moreover the law entered that the
offense might abound. But where sin
abounded, grace abounded much more, so
that as sin reigned in death, even so grace
might reign through righteousness to eternal
life through Jesus Christ our Lord.*
Romans 5:17-21 (NKJV)

It began to dawn on me! "I am no longer under Adam! I am under Jesus Christ! Fear and anxiety have no place in my life!" I must kick them out and replace them with the truths in God's Word! A great example of kicking those tormenting twins (fear and anxiety) out and replacing them with God's Truth, is what I previously mentioned. Know and recognize that God is our **Peace**! Begin right now, even as you are reading this. Pause, and realize and personalize this truth for yourself. Say aloud, "*Yahweh Shalom-The Lord is my Peace.* He is also my prosperity, completeness, soundness and total welfare! Fear and anxiety, you must GO!"

Chapter 3 - When Truths Become Reality

With a foundation properly laid that Christ is our Peace and that we are no longer under Adam; hence, no longer under fear, we are ready to unfold 2 Timothy 1:7.

For God has not given us a spirit of fear, but
of power and of love and of a sound mind.
2 Timothy 1:7 (NKJV)

If you study the Books of 1 and 2 Timothy, you will see a very young Timothy not only had the responsibility of pastoring the church at Ephesus, but also of facing the severe persecution of Christians under Nero. Commentators agree that Timothy appears to have been vacillating. He was constitutionally timid. But Paul exhorts him: God's Spirit does <u>not</u> make you fearful - just the opposite. God's Spirit, the Holy Spirit makes you strong, brave, and unafraid!

=== THE SPIRIT OF FEAR ===

Christ makes fearless men.

- A MacLaren-

Fear (spirit of) is from the Greek word *deilia* which means terror, dread, craven and cringing. The Holy Spirit is not one that shrinks from danger. He does not leave you craven and cringing, ambivalent, and wavering with fear, doubt, and unbelief. Rather, as previously stated, the Holy Spirit makes you strong, brave, and unafraid!

The Holy Spirit is within you! Pull on His strength! Ask Him to show you 'how' to be brave in any given situation!

=== POWER ===

*But you shall receive power when the Holy
Spirit has come upon you; and you shall
be witnesses to Me in Jerusalem, and in all
Judea and Samaria, and to the end of the
earth.*
Acts 1:8 (NKJV)

*...And they chose Stephen, a man full of faith
and the Holy Spirit...*
Acts 6:5 (NKJV)

*Therefore do not be ashamed of the testimony
of our Lord, nor of me His prisoner, but
share with me in the sufferings for the gospel
according to the power of God,*
2 Timothy 1:8 (NKJV)

Power is from the Greek word *Dunamis* and it means miraculous power, might, and strength. Think dynamite, with all its explosive energy. When you belong to God and are filled with his Spirit, you are no longer running on y*our* power. You are running on *His* power. (Crucial truth!) Power is the invariable accompaniment of the gift of the Holy Spirit. ***He gave us His power to overcome fear.***

This power enables you to face the enemy victoriously, bear up under trials, and triumph in persecutions.

This power is yours. Know it. Receive it.
Walk in it. Use it.

----

*For God has not given us a spirit of fear, but of power and of **love** and of a sound mind.*
2 Timothy 1:7 (NKJV)

=== LOVE ===

For God so loved the world that He gave His only begotten Son, that whoever believes in Him should not perish but have everlasting life.
John 3:16 (NKJV)

Agápē love is the highest form of love. *Agápē* love originates from God or Christ for mankind. This is the BEST news! This is the revelation that I so desperately needed at the beginning of my journey. Somehow I had gotten the crazy, WRONG idea that the more I did, or the better I performed a task, the happier God would be with me. I was on some kind of an 'earn brownie points in heaven in order to please God' system. I was so WRONG! Nothing could be further from the truth. As I continued to spend increased amounts of time with God in those early years, (after the final plate came crashing down that I spoke of in Chapter 1), I learned that God's love is not based on any kind of condition, (whether you perform well or not.) It is not based on what other people say about you or what you say about yourself. **God loves you simply because He loves you!** It is not duty but desire on His part. I just cannot shout this enough times! Please receive it! **God loves YOU!** *The revelation of God's agape love and the security that this revelation brings drives out all fear!*

*For God has not given us a spirit of fear, but of power and of love and of a **<u>sound mind</u>**.*
2 Timothy 1:7 (NKJV)

=== SOUND MIND ===

Sóphronismos is the Greek word for sound mind. In the Bible, it is used only in this verse and it means "wise discretion." With the Holy Spirit at work in you, you are sensible and well balanced with a sound mind and good judgment. ***Through Him, you have the ability to have disciplined thinking.***

God gives you what you need - the power, love and ability to think clearly to maintain a productive, victorious life. (More on this in the next chapter.)

How to Apply What You Have Learned So Far

Get alone with God.
> *Let us therefore come boldly to the throne of grace, that we may obtain mercy and find grace to help in time of need.*
Hebrews 4:16 (NKJV)

Remember your covenant of peace.

From the vantage point of peace, begin to converse with God regarding the area of fear with which you are struggling. Remember to keep your eyes on Christ and not on the fear. **If you focus on the fear, you empower the fear and doubt. If you focus on Jesus, you empower faith. God has given you Divine power to shift your focus.**

> *Be anxious for nothing, but in everything by*
> *prayer and supplication, with thanksgiving,*
> *let your requests be made known to*
> *God; and the peace of God, which surpasses*
> *all understanding, will guard your hearts*
> *and minds through Christ Jesus.*
> Philippians 4:6-7 (NKJV)

Get a vision.

Envision what your life would look like if you were so secure that you *could* operate in 'power, love and a sound mind'. God will help you with this vision and, also, help make that vision become a reality.

Find scriptural truths that address the area(s) you are facing.

The scriptures addressing the situation may not seem capable of conquering the problem at first glance. But, as you continue watering them, nurturing them, protecting them, and applying them, their power will grow.

If you are persistent, those Scriptures will cast out the nagging lies of fear. But, you must hold fast to those power-filled words of God! You are established in Christ. Line up your thinking with His truths. (More on this in Chapter 4.)

> *Finally, brethren, whatever is true, whatever is honorable, whatever is right, whatever is pure, whatever is lovely, whatever is of good repute, if there is any excellence and if anything worthy of praise, dwell on these things.*
> Philippians 4:8 (NKJV)

Pray and fast.

> *Is this not the fast that I have chosen: To loose the bonds of wickedness...*
> Isaiah 58:6 (NKJV)

> *However, this kind does not go out except by prayer and fasting.*
> Matthew 17:21 (NKJV)

Remember there is power in the Name of Jesus.

Allow God to fill you anew with His power to overcome.

Remember that Jesus is in you!

*...teaching them to observe all things that I
have commanded you; and lo, I am with you
always, even to the end of the age....*
Matthew 28:20 (NKJV)

*Whenever I am afraid, I will trust in You. In
God (I will praise His word), in God I have
put my trust; I will not fear. What can flesh
do to me?*
Psalms 56:3-4 (NKJV)

*Behold, God is my salvation, I will trust and
not be afraid; 'For Yah, the Lord, is my
strength and song; He also has become my
salvation.'*
Isaiah 12:2 (NKJV)

Chapter 4 - Eleven Ways to Renew the Mind

As we saw in the first three chapters, it is our right and privilege to be functioning with a sound, disciplined mind. In keeping with that truth, and in order to do this, we must always continue to do what the Apostle Paul describes as 'renewing the mind'.

And do not be conformed to this world, but be transformed by the renewing of your mind, so that you may prove what the will of God is, that which is good and acceptable and perfect.
Romans 12:2 (NKJV)

and be renewed in the spirit of your mind,
Ephesians 4:23 (NKJV)

What is wrong with the human mind?
Why does it have to be renewed?

The problem with our minds is not merely that we are finite, and don't have all the information. The problem is that our minds are fallen. They have a spirit, a bent, a mindset that is hostile to the absolute supremacy of God. Our minds are bent on not seeing God as infinitely more worthy of praise than we are, or the things we make or achieve.

- John Piper

Until our minds are renewed and brought under the Lordship of Jesus Christ, our thought life can run rampant with unhealthy, uncontrolled thinking! The results can be catastrophic!

The good news is this - we *can* win the battle in our minds! God has given us everything we will ever need to win! We have the Word of God, the blood of Christ, praise, worship, grace and the precious Holy Spirit to help us, undergird us and guide us as we embark on renewing our minds!

Therefore if the Son makes you free, you shall be free indeed.
John 8:36 (NKJV)

Thanks to Jesus, and the price He paid at the cross for us; our minds can once again be sharp, clear, healthy, whole, and full of peace!

I have listed eleven ways to 'Renew the Mind' in this chapter. But before we get to those, let's take a brief look at what 'renewing our minds' really means. To 'renew our minds' is not simply 'changing what we think' by using our own self-effort and/or thoughts. But as we see in Ephesians 4:22-24, we are actually doing an exchange.

We are 'putting off' our old corrupt thinking and 'exchanging' it for 'new, saved redeemed' thinking according to the Word of God!

Strip yourselves of your former nature [put
off and discard your old unrenewed self]
which characterized your previous manner of
life and becomes corrupt through
lusts and desires that spring from delusion;
And be constantly renewed in the spirit of
your mind [having a fresh mental and
spiritual attitude],
And put on the new nature (the regenerate
self) created in God's image, [Godlike] in
true righteousness and holiness.
Ephesians 4:22-24 (AMPC)

Additional definitions of 'being renewed' (in the spirit of your mind) are:

Jamieson-Fausset-Brown Bible Commentary:
be renewed—The Greek (*ananeousthai*) implies "the <u>continued renewal in the youth of the new man</u>." A different Greek word (*anakainousthai*) implies "<u>renewal from the old state</u>." [Underline added for emphasis]

Gill's Exposition of the Entire Bible:
And be renewed in the spirit of your mind—Or by the Spirit that is in your mind; that is, by the Holy Spirit; Who is in the saints, and is the Author of renovation in them; and Who is the Reviver and Carrier on, and Finisher of that work, and therefore that is called the renewing of the Holy Spirit.

> The Spirit renews the mind. It is first and decisively His work. We are radically dependent on Him. Our efforts follow His initiatives and enablings.
>
> - John Piper

This is what transforms our lives. A renewed mind is one whose thought life has come under the Lordship of Jesus Christ. A renewed mind is under the government of Jesus Christ, at peace without turmoil or anxiety.

Behavior, actions, and lifestyles-begin in the mind. They cannot be changed with a snap of the finger. It takes ***mind renewal*** to affect permanent change. The renewal of the mind will allow us to receive wisdom from the Holy Spirit that will cause us to prosper in any circumstance.

These next eleven steps are the fundamentals that I have compiled and put into practice in order to renew the mind and maintain a sound mind. (Or, in Beth Moore's words: Reclaim, Replace, and Renew our minds!)

Eleven Ways to Renew the Mind

1. Re-surrender Your Life to the Lord.

So he answered and said, " 'You shall love the Lord your God with all your heart, with all your soul, with all your strength, and with all your mind,' and 'your neighbor as yourself.' "

Luke 10:27 (NKJV)

It takes a conscious effort and spiritual discipline for you to present yourself to the Lord. Spend quiet time with Him. Re-surrender, re-submit, re-align your mind, will and emotions with and to the purposes of God.

2. Listen/Hear the Word of God.

Be aware of what you are listening to. What you listen to affects you. Guard your ears; they are the "eargate".

- John Piper

So then faith comes by hearing, and hearing by the Word of God.

Romans 10:17 (NKJV)

What are you hearing? What are you listening to?

3. Read Your Bible.

Search for Christ. Search for revelations. Search for Scriptural truths concerning the areas of struggle you are facing. Search for truths that renew and transform your mind and your life. Truly study your Bible. The Scriptures were not given for our information, but for our transformation.

-D.L. Moody

There are differences in 'Informational Reading' and 'Formational Reading' of Scripture. [4]

Informational Reading	**Formational Reading**
Seeks to cover as much as possible	Focuses on small portions
A linear process	An in-depth process
Seeks to master the text	Allows the text to master us
The text as an object to use	The text as a subject that shapes us
Analytical, critical, and judgmental approach	Humble, submissive, willing, loving approach
Problem-solving mentality	Openness to mystery

*Open my eyes, that I may see wondrous
things from Your law.*
Psalms 119:18 (NKJV)

*All Scripture is God-breathed [given by
divine inspiration] and is profitable for
instruction, for conviction [of sin], for
correction [of error and restoration to
obedience], for training in righteousness
[learning to live in conformity to God's will,
both publicly and privately—
behaving honorably with personal integrity
and moral courage]...*
2 Timothy 3:16 (AMP)

*Show me Your ways, O Lord; Teach me Your
paths. Lead me in Your truth and teach me,
For You are the God of my salvation; On You
I wait all the day.*
Psalms 25:4-5 (NKJV)

4. Meditate on the Word of God.
Form a Habit of Meditating. Chew, Ask, and Ponder.

*The law of his God is in his heart; None of
his steps shall slide.*
Psalms 37:31 (NKJV)

Finally, brethren, whatever things are true,
whatever things are noble, whatever
things are just, whatever things are pure,
whatever things are lovely, whatever
things are of good report, if there is any
virtue and if there is anything praiseworthy—
meditate on these things.
Philippians 4:8 (NKJV)

Let the word of Christ dwell in you richly in
all wisdom;...
Colossians 3:16 (NKJV)

The word *meditate* literally means "to mutter," which implies continually speaking God's Word to yourself. **Meditation will increase your ability to believe.** God's Word is digested in the mind. Then, it passes into the heart and spirit. Just as it takes time for food to digest and become part of your body, so it takes time for the Word of God to digest into your soul. That is why meditation on the Word cannot be rushed. The ***key is to meditate on the Word*** until it becomes part of your everyday behavior.

If you want to have the 'mind of Christ', you must frequently shut the door to EVERY other distraction in your life and get alone with Him because God does not and will not yell; He speaks in a still, soft, voice.
- Beth Moore

5. Speak God's Word Aloud.

Speaking the Word of God aloud is a powerful, Biblical principle that accomplishes many things.

It helps you to keep the Word of God alive in your heart.

It helps your faith to grow. Your spirit man hears the truth, thus causing your faith to grow and stay strong. "So then faith comes by *hearing*, and *hearing* by the Word of God. (Romans 10:17, NKJV) [Italics added for emphasis]

The Word can be applied like **medicine**. "My son, give attention to my words; Incline your ear to my sayings. Do not let them depart from your eyes; Keep them in the midst of your heart; For they are life to those who find them, And **health** to all their flesh." (Proverbs 4:20-22, NKJV) [Bold and italics added for emphasis] There is a footnote in the KJV of the Bible that shows that the word **health** in this verse means **medicine**.

When struggling with a problem, speak the Word of God aloud that applies to that situation. You will bring life and truth to it!

Speak the Word of God aloud if you are having a hard time thinking correctly. Every time a thought comes to your mind that does not agree with God's Word, or puts you into confusion, despair or fear, declare the Scriptural truth aloud against that wrong thought. You will find the wrong thought disappearing. What you are literally doing when you do this is blocking or eradicating the ability for the wrong thought to continue down its familiar pathway in your mind. You are stopping it in its tracks! But here is a huge key: You must then REPLACE that wrong thought with the CORRECT thought/truth from the Word of God. You will then be creating a new pathway for your new thought to travel!

If the enemy has been able to lodge a *stronghold* in your mind, (**Stronghold-** Biblically - any idea, thought, principle, argument or reasoning contrary to GOD's Word. It **holds strong** in your mind, not wanting to let go), one of the most powerful things you can do to **demolish** that *stronghold*, is to speak the Word of God (that addresses that stronghold) over (and into) that situation. "For the weapons of our warfare are not physical [weapons of flesh and blood], *but they are mighty before God for the overthrow and destruction of strongholds*, [Inasmuch as we] refute arguments *and* theories *and* reasonings and every proud *and* lofty thing that sets itself up against the [true] knowledge of God; and we lead every thought *and* purpose away captive into the obedience of Christ (the

Messiah, the Anointed One)" *(2* Corinthians 10:4-5, AMPC) [Bold and italics added for emphasis]

Speak and pray the Scriptural truths over and over until you experience absolute and lasting freedom. Be firm. You are not trying to manage the stronghold; you are out to demolish it! *(See "Speaking God's Word" in the back of this book for some examples of Scriptural truths for you to speak and pray.)*

God's Word is a Sword! It is the Sword of the Spirit! It is double-edged. "For the word of God is living and powerful, and sharper than any two-edged sword." (Hebrews 4:12, NKJV) As one Bible teacher says, "One edge builds your faith, while the other defeats the devil".

Another Bible teacher continues: The power of the Word of God is enough to create worlds and defeat devils. The weapon with which the devil is defeated is the Word of God. When we speak the Word, we are speaking Christ into that situation.

As you continue to speak the Word of God aloud over your life, believing what it says, you are setting yourself in agreement with God and for His plan to come to pass in your life. Begin to declare the Word of God over your life until you see your situation change and it begins to 'look like' what you see in God's Word. Jeremiah 23:29 describes the Word as being like a fire and a hammer!

"Is not My word like a fire?" says the Lord,
"And like a hammer that breaks the rock in
pieces?"
Jeremiah 23:29 (NKJV)

God's Word backed by God's Power and God's Holy Spirit, will 'break' or 'burn' that thing that you are facing and replace it with the victory given in God's Word!

6. Apply the Word of God!

After you are *listening/hearing* the Word of God (#2), *reading* the Word of God (#3), *meditating* on the Word of God (#4), and *speaking* God's Word aloud (#5), you are now ready to *apply* the Word of God!

If you intend to profit by the Word, bring it home to yourself: A medicine will do no good unless it be applied.

- John Piper

There comes a point where all of the study, memorizing, and declaration of the Word of God has to be 'acted upon.' You eventually must begin to take steps 'toward' that 'thing' that has kept you back. Shift your focus from that 'thing' and onto Jesus. As you do, you will see that 'thing' getting smaller and the strength that comes from Jesus getting larger. You are becoming equipped. You are full of God, His love and His Word. Take a step. Go forward in Jesus' name. All of heaven is backing you!

> *But be doers of the word, and not hearers*
> *only, ...*
> James 1:22 (NKJV)

> *But do you want to know, O foolish man, that*
> *faith without works is dead?*
> James 2:20 (NKJV)

> *As you therefore have received Christ Jesus*
> *the Lord, so walk in Him, rooted and built up*
> *in Him and established in the faith, as you*
> *have been taught, abounding in it with*
> *thanksgiving.*
> Colossians 2:6-7 (NKJV)

7. Reckon yourself as dead to old desires.

Do not feed your old desires. Feed your newborn spirit that now lives on the inside of you. Recognize the gains you have in Christ's love. Compare these to the empty promises offered by desires of the flesh.

> *Likewise you also, reckon yourselves to*
> *be dead indeed to sin, but alive to God in*
> *Christ Jesus our Lord.*
> Romans 6:11 (NKJV)

8. Halt negative conditioning from your past.

Recognize negative conditioning from your past. If you do not, you will simply repeat the past. If you see any negative conditioning, reprogram with the truth.

Finally, brethren, whatever things are true,
whatever things are noble, whatever
things are just, whatever things are pure,
whatever things are lovely, whatever
things are of good report, if there is any
virtue and if there is anything praiseworthy—
meditate on these things.
Philippians 4:8 (NKJV)

9. Pray.

Simply talk with God. To fully realize God's will, you must pray (talk with God).

Be anxious for nothing, but in everything by
prayer and supplication, with thanksgiving,
let your requests be made known to
God; and the peace of God, which surpasses
all understanding, will guard your hearts
and minds through Christ Jesus.
Philippians 4:6-7 (NKJV)

10. Resist conformity to the world.

Do not be conformed, but be transformed by the renewing of the mind.

And do not be conformed to this world,
but be transformed by the renewing of your
mind...
Romans 12:2 (NKJV)

Don't become so well-adjusted to your
culture that you fit into it without even
thinking. Instead, fix your attention on God.
You'll be changed from the inside out.
Readily recognize what he wants from you,
and quickly respond to it. Unlike the culture
around you, always dragging you down to its
level of immaturity, God brings the best out
of you, develops well-formed maturity in you.
Romans 12:2 (MSG)

Don't copy the behavior and customs of this
world, but let God transform you into a new
person by changing the way you think. Then
you will learn to know God's will for you,
which is good and pleasing and perfect.
Romans 12:2 (NLT)

11. Recharge your spiritual batteries.

God infuses new energy, vitality, and ideas to our minds when we are renewed by His Word, His Holy Spirit, and fellowship with other believers. You cannot get very far when you simply coast. (Picture coasting; you eventually stop!)

Recharging your spiritual batteries for effective mind renewal is crucial! How to recharge? One of the best ways is to do what the Psalmist says in the verses below. "*Lift your eyes up to the Lord!*" Run to God! Your help comes from Him! Take the time to sit and just saturate in the Lord's Presence. This will do so much with regards to helping you have the wherewithal to renew your mind! Psalm 121:1-7-is one of my favorite Psalms! Let's look at it together!

I will lift up my eyes to the hills—
From whence comes my help?
My help comes from the Lord,
Who made heaven and earth.
He will not allow your foot to be moved;
He who keeps you will not slumber.
Behold, He who keeps Israel
Shall neither slumber nor sleep.
The Lord is your keeper;
The Lord is your shade at your right hand.
The sun shall not strike you by day,
Nor the moon by night.
The Lord shall preserve you from all evil;
He shall preserve your soul.
Psalm 121:1-7 (NKJV)

While in the atmosphere of God's Presence, His Word can come alive to you once again! The Holy Spirit can bring you the comfort that you have been waiting for!

Other suggestions for recharging your spiritual batteries for effective mind renewal, can be:

~Worship. Put on your favorite worship music! Really allow yourself to enjoy it and enter into God's Presence with it!

~How about enjoying a hobby or a talent or a gift that God has given you. Do you love to garden? Are you a painter? Go for it!

~Maybe simply taking a wonderful nap or sitting and reading, will help you to recharge.

~Taking long walks and breathing in God's fresh air, and enjoying His amazing creation can help you calm your thoughts, and enter into His rest.

~Sit and have a fabulous lunch or a cup of coffee or a cup of tea with a wonderful friend. Maybe it is time to reconnect and fellowship with long lost friends.

Whatever you feel drawn to do, in order to intentionally help get your mind in the right zone (strong, renewed, full of peace, disciplined thinking, free from anxiety, fear and other destructive thinking), make sure you carve out the needed time and do it!

Release Your Faith...God's Word Works!

Chapter 5 - The Power of a Seed

I wanted to insert this important chapter entitled, *The Power of a Seed*,[5] to encourage you that everything we have been learning thus far, has landed into our hearts and minds, in *seed* form.

As many of you have already discovered, reading the precious truths from God's Word, making them yours, and seeing the fruit or the manifestation of those truths operative in your lives, takes time! But hang in there! It does happen!

Kingdom Parable

*And He said, "The kingdom of God is as if a
man should scatter seed on the ground, and
should sleep by night and rise by day, and
the seed should sprout and grow, he himself
does not know how. For the earth yields
crops by itself: first the blade, then the head,
after that the full grain in the head. But when
the grain ripens, immediately he puts in the
sickle, because the harvest has come."*
Mark 4:26-29 (NKJV)

Please notice in this Parable from Jesus that Jesus describes *how* The Kingdom of God works! "...first the blade, then the head, after that the full grain in the head. But when the grain ripens, immediately he puts in the sickle, because the harvest has come." (Mark 4:28-29, NKJV) This is such a great, practical illustration of faith!

Just prior to these passages, in Mark 4:2-20, Jesus tells the Parable of the *seeds* and the soils. In that Parable, Jesus explains that *Seed* is the Word of God and the good soil is a receptive heart. A receptive heart hears the Word of God, holds it fast, and bears fruit.

Jesus was referring to the Word of God as *Seed* in the Gospel of Mark, and Peter refers to the Word of God as *Seed* in 1 Peter 1:23.

> *having been born again, not of corruptible*
> *seed but incorruptible, through the word of*
> *God which lives and abides forever,*
>
> 1 Peter 1:23 (NKJV)

James also refers to the Word of God as *Seed* in James 1:21.

> *...receive the word [of God] which is*
> *implanted [actually **rooted in your heart**],*
> *which is able to save your souls.*
>
> James 1:21 (AMP)
> [Bold added for emphasis]

*...humbly accept the word **planted in
you**, which can save you.*

James 1:21 (NIV)
[Bold added for emphasis]

The literal picture is that of planting a *seed* in the ground. The figurative picture, as used by James, is of the *seed* of the Word of God being planted in the heart where it takes root. It begins within you in *seed* form.

Paul also refers to the Word of God as *Seed* in 1 Corinthians 3:6.

*I planted the **seed**, Apollos watered it, but
God has been making it grow.*

1 Corinthians 3:6 (NIV)
[Bold added for emphasis]

In this chapter, the Word of God will also be referred to as *Seed*.

The principle of the *seed* can be seen throughout Scripture. You see its early beginnings in the Book of Genesis.

*Then God said, "Let the earth bring forth
grass, the herb that yields **seed**, and the fruit
tree that yields fruit according to its kind,
whose **seed** is in itself, on the earth"; and it
was so. And the earth brought forth grass,
the herb that yields **seed** according to its
kind, and the tree that yields fruit, whose
seed is in itself according to its kind. And
God saw that it was good.*

Genesis 1:11-12 (NKJV)
[Bold added for emphasis]

The word *seed* is the Greek word *sperma*. That gives us a lot of insight to the nature of *seed*. It is the *sperma*. It is the thing that brings conception and life to the situation. When the sperm and the egg meet, something happens. Conception takes place. That is where life begins. The *seed* is the image of the harvest. Think about it using the illustration of an acorn and an oak tree. That tiny acorn has within it the DNA to potentially become a mighty oak! That is a natural illustration. Can you imagine what the *seed* of the Word of God will produce on the inside of us! If you will dare to sow that Word on the good ground of your heart it will produce the image that is in the seed.

As I stated earlier, I felt it very important to insert this chapter of *The Power of a Seed*. Even the title is a teaching all on its own! *The Power of a Seed* is worth remembering! Here's why: Though I see the truths written in Scripture for a sound mind, freedom from anxiety and other destructive thinking, I have to realize that those truths will land in my heart and my mind in *seed* form. I must then water those *seeds*, (meditate upon them, keep them in front of me, get them way down on the inside of me), and tend to them.

Why is the 'Seed' so powerful?

That *Seed* is so powerful because that *Seed* is Jesus Himself! He is alive! That *Seed* is alive! You cannot separate the two, which makes this all the more powerful and exciting! When you are beholding the Word of God, you are beholding Jesus!

*In the beginning was the Word, and the Word was with God, and the **Word was God.***

John 1:1 (NKJV)
[Bold added for emphasis]

And the Word became flesh and dwelt among us, and we beheld His glory, the glory as of the only begotten of the Father, full of grace and truth.

John 1:14 (NKJV)

How the *seed* operates.

Seeds do not grow sitting in a sack on your shelf. They must be planted in the proper place. Every *seed* is powerless unless it is planted. In Mark 4:15, 16, 18, 20, it stated that the *Seed* is planted by **hearing** it. According to Romans 10:17, faith comes by **hearing** and **hearing** by the Word of God. You must **hear** it and **hear** it and **hear** it, again, until it registers in your spirit. *Seeds* must germinate! That husk (hard exterior) surrounding your *seed* must break! Once broken, the seed then can find its home (in the soft soil of your heart!).

Hearing and abiding is a posture before God. How long do you have to hear it? As Joe Purcell says, "How badly do you want it? How long? Until revelation comes. Until that *Seed* sprouts and grows and makes your way prosperous."

A *seed* is much smaller than the plant it produces.

The problem you face may seem huge. In comparison, a Scripture may seem very small. But when planted, that *seed* will grow in you and overcome the problem. Never forget: In the Word of God, there is a *seed* (Scriptural Truth) for every need.

A *seed* is powerful.

As a *seed* begins to grow, it will push up dirt, rocks, etc. Whatever the obstacles are, God's Word ***planted in your heart*** will push obstacles out of the way.

A *seed* takes time to produce.

No one expects a *seed* to produce a harvest the same day that *seed* is planted. (Remember Mark 4:26-29: first the blade, then the head, after that the full grain in the head) With every *seed*, there is a period of time where it looks like nothing is happening! The ground looks dormant! Do not expect instantaneous results. The timing issue, when you are in faith, does not matter. That *seed* is growing!

A *seed* produces after its own kind.

Apple *seeds* produce apples. Orange *seeds* produce oranges. When the Word of God is planted within your heart, and it begins to take root, once acted upon, the ***image*** on the inside of that *seed* (Scripture), or that Scripture will begin to grow up on the inside of you and produce the very DNA lying on the inside of that *seed*.

A *seed* is persistent.

A *seed* is very persistent! *Seeds* work! A *seed* never gives up, but works day and night. Even when you are sleeping, the *seed* you have planted is working to grow and express itself in a fruitful harvest if you have nurtured that *seed*.

> *...should sleep by night and rise by day, and the seed should sprout and grow, he himself does not know how.*
>
> Mark 4:27 (NKJV)

A *seed* will stop growing without nourishment.

Simply planting a *seed* is not enough to assure a harvest, however. *Seed* must be protected and taken care of until harvest time. A *seed* that is dug up or not watered will not produce.

In consistency lies the power!

This law of *seed*time and harvest operates in every area of our lives. If we will plant God's Word in our hearts, then allow the *seed* to germinate and the plant to grow to maturity, we will reap the fruit of a harvest. Always remember, *in **consistency**, lies the power!* Think about how consistent natural *seed* is. Now, think about how consistent the supernatural imperishable seed of God's Word is. Properly planted and cared for, ***it will produce every time***.

While the earth remains,
Seed*time and harvest,*
Cold and heat,
Winter and summer,
And day and night
Shall not cease.
Genesis 8:22 (NKJV)
[Bold added for emphasis]

Closing Remarks

I am beyond excited for you as you begin to take the truths from this book and apply them to your own life!

It has been nearly three decades since I first faced, learned about, and sought Biblically based solutions to anxiety, fear, and any other destructive thinking. I have learned that God was, and is, there for me every step of the way. He will be there for you, as well!

Never give up! To this day, there are times when anxiety will try to grip me, once again. But as I have been sharing, I quickly apply the truths from the Word of God and the anxiety soon flees.

Jesus paid the highest price imaginable for our sound mind and freedom. He gave His own life.

I cheer you on! Freedom from anxiety, fear and other destructive thinking can be yours! Begin to study and apply what you have learned today!

Speaking God's Word

If you are feeling **anxious**,
>   read meditate on, and speak aloud:
Psalms 86:7
Proverbs 3:5-6
John 14:27
Philippians 4:6-7
2 Timothy 1:7
1 Peter 5:6-7

If you are feeling **worry**,
>   read meditate on, and speak aloud:
Isaiah 26:4
Matthew 6:27
Matthew 6:34
John 14:27
Philippians 4:6-7
Colossians 3:15
2 Timothy 1:7

If you are feeling **fear**,
		read meditate on, and speak aloud:
Psalms 27:1
Psalms 56:3-4
Romans 8:15
John 14:1
John 14:27
2 Timothy 1:7

If you are feeling **hopeless**,
		read meditate on, and speak aloud:
Psalms 25:4-5
Psalms 27:13-14
Jeremiah 29:11
Lamentations 3:20-24
Romans 5:5
Romans 15:13
Hebrews 4:16
1 Peter 5:6-7

Salvation Through Christ

*Jesus answered and said to him, "Most
assuredly, I say to you, unless one is
born again, he cannot see the kingdom of
God." Nicodemus said to Him, "How can a
man be born when he is old? Can he enter a
second time into his mother's womb and be
born?" Jesus answered, "Most assuredly, I
say to you, unless one is born of water and
the Spirit, he cannot enter the kingdom of
God. That which is born of the flesh is flesh,
and that which is born of the Spirit is spirit.*
John 3:3-6 (NKJV)

The Bible says, "For all have sinned and come short of the glory of God." (Romans 3:23, NKJV) When Adam sinned in the Garden, sin came into the world. This separated man from God. But Christ Jesus came to undo that separation - to reunite man, once again, to God Almighty. Jesus did this by dying on the cross for our sins and rising again from the grave. He made the way possible for us to once again be united with our Heavenly Father and live forever with Him in heaven.

Salvation is a free gift from God. We receive this free gift when we believe and trust in the Lord Jesus Christ. We must trust Jesus Christ and ask Him into our hearts to save us from eternal destruction - to bridge that separation due to sin, to reunite us with the Father...to be our Lord and our Savior.

*...if you confess with your mouth the Lord
Jesus and believe in your heart that God has
raised Him from the dead, you will be
saved. For with
the heart one believes unto righteousness,
and with the mouth confession is made unto
salvation.*
Romans 10:9-10 (NKJV)

*"And this is the will of Him who sent
Me, that everyone who sees the Son and
believes in Him may have everlasting life;
and I will raise him up at the last day."*
John 6:40 (NKJV)

*"He who believes in the Son has eternal life;
but he who does not obey the Son shall not
see life, but the wrath of God abides on
him."*
John 3:36 (NKJV)

The Bible says that there is salvation in no other…

*Jesus said to him, "I am the way, the truth,
and the life. No one comes to the
Father except through Me.*
John 14:6 (NKJV)

Nor is there salvation in any other, for there is no other name under heaven given among men by which we must be saved.

Acts 4:12 (NKJV)

Salvation Prayer

Lord Jesus, I know that I am a sinner. I recognize my need for a Savior. I am so sorry for my sins. I believe that You died on the cross for me and that You rose from the dead. I ask You to forgive me now. Please come into my heart and be my Lord and Savior. I want to know You! I love You! Thank You for saving me.

Congratulations - Welcome to the family of God. If you have any questions or if we can be of any assistance, please contact us at:

Anna Donahue Ministries
PO Box 644
Destrehan, La. 70047

administries@cox.net

(504) 451-4804

Sources

1, 2, 3 Kenneth Copeland Ministries

4 M. Robert Mulholland, Jr as presented by Kenneth Boa in *Conformed to His Image*

5   Joe Purcell Ministries   Some of the thoughts in this chapter are based in part upon a sermon by Rev. Joseph Purcell, entitled "The Power of a Seed." Used by permission. The phrase "Seed is powerless until it is planted" is from F. F. Bosworth, <u>Christ the Healer</u>, 9th Ed. (Grand Rapids, MI: Fleming H. Revell, 2000), Location 107, 1608. Kindle Ed.

Bible Verses to Cut Out & Carry With You

If you want to print additional cards,
see the link or QR code below:

http://annadonahueministries.com/bibleverses.html

For God has not given us a spirit of fear, but of power and of love and of a sound mind.
2 Timothy 1:7 (NKJV)

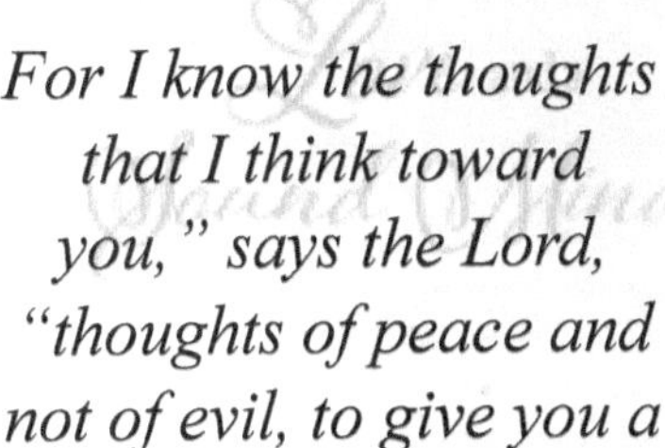

For I know the thoughts that I think toward you," says the Lord, "thoughts of peace and not of evil, to give you a future and a hope.
Jeremiah 29:11 (NKJV)

Be anxious for nothing, but in everything by prayer and supplication, with thanksgiving, let your requests be made known to God; and the peace of God, which surpasses all understanding, will guard your hearts and minds through Christ Jesus.
Philippians 4:6-7 (NKJV)

Finally, brethren, whatever is true, whatever is honorable, whatever is right, whatever is pure, whatever is lovely, whatever is of good repute, if there is any excellence and if anything worthy of praise, dwell on these things.
Philippians 4:8 (NASB)

In the day of my
trouble I will call upon
You,
For You will answer
me.
Psalms 86:7 (NKJV)

Trust in the Lord with
all your heart,
And lean not on your
own understanding;
In all your ways
acknowledge Him,
And He shall direct
your paths.
Proverbs 3:5-6 (NKJV)

For you did not receive
the spirit of bondage
again to fear, but you
received the Spirit of
adoption by whom we cry
out, "Abba, Father."
Romans 8:15 (NKJV)

My soul still remembers
And sinks within me.
This I recall to my mind,
Therefore I have hope.
Through the Lord's mercies we
are not consumed,
Because His compassions fail
not.
They are new every morning;
Great is Your faithfulness.
"The Lord is my portion,"
says my soul,
"Therefore I hope in Him!"
Lamentations 3:20-24 (NKJV)